My Encounter With Ordinary Women Who Led Extraordinary Lives

My Encounter With Ordinary Women Who Led Extraordinary Lives

As Torchbearers of Culture, Way Showers of Self-Determination and Freedom

Bernard W. Saunders

To order additional copies of this book, contact:
Xlibris Corporation
1-888-795-4274
www.Xlibris.com
Orders@Xlibris.com
95249

CONTENTS

Introduction..9

Lil 13
Charshee Charlotte Lawrence McIntyre 21
Marjorie Ransom 26
Sarah Buntin Payne...31
Sybil Williams Clarke...39
Doris Viola (Hobson) Osborne 47

Epilogue...53
Postscript..57

My thanks to Katherine "Kitty" Chavis, the daughter of Doris Osborne, for allowing the use of her art ("Emos Children" ©) for the cover (E-mail: *Kandicreations@hotmail.com*), and to my friend Dorothy Ross for the overall design of the cover. Also my friend, Diane Richardison Lyons, who edited *Women*.

Introduction

I have known—been blessed to have known—many wondrous women in my life: women of color, ordinary women by most standards born to humble circumstances, who achieved, in my judgment, extraordinary things, given the obstacles of race, gender, class, and male chauvinism they faced as women of color in an often hostile society.

Those written of here are generally of the same age group, and although of different cultural backgrounds, the similarities in their heritage bind them together. Their longevity was, in itself, in many instances, a testimony to their will.

I would also argue that their struggles to make ends meet and the contributions of the men (for good or bad) in their lives are analogous to most people I have known in my lifetime. History supports that these women are also representative of people of color since they first made contact with persons of European descent.

As individuals and as a people still under duress, from within and without, we need to take to heart the gift these women have given us by their willingness to open up and to share their lives with us so that we may learn from them as they have learned from others who came before them.

I am honored to introduce you to the six of them, who, in my judgment, embody women of color who are torchbearers of culture and therefore way showers of self-determination and freedom. These women were—are—bereft of any feelings or thoughts of racial or gender victimization. While experiencing both, they refused to allow the pathologies of the United States and other societies to keep them from achieving self-determination.

They are Lillian Belle Miles Saunders, Charshee Charlotte, Lawrence McIntyre, Marjorie Ransom, Sarah Buntin Payne, Sybil Williams Clark, and Doris Osborne.

To our collective ancestors I pour a symbolic libation. To the ancestors, the six women mentioned above, and all of the other women who they are metaphors of, I give thanks for giving me this opportunity to serve.

I would be remiss if I did not give thanks to my friend, Jane Payne Saunders, who, though of another generation, embodies many of the same qualities of the subjects written about here, who read and reread the manuscript as it evolved from audio tapes through many drafts with great patience, often offering suggestions from her deep well of spiritual intuitiveness that added insights that I would have missed otherwise.

The same can be said of Sister Diane Richardson-Lyons, whose creative editing enhanced this work immeasurably, as well as my sister in struggle, Lori Andrews, who overcame the technical difficulties that I couldn't in completing the manuscript.

Kudos are also due to my son Milton Bernard Saunders, whose skills with computer imaging and his photographer's eye reproduced many of the pictures in this work from an assortment of photographs, some from unknown photographers who also deserve my thanks.

His brother, Christopher Wade Saunders, in turn, took the photographs and produced the wonderful pencil sketches of the primary subjects that have enhanced the overall quality of this production, for he has captured their essence in his art.

That this is the first collaboration between myself, my two sons, and our extended family on something of this nature adds to my sense of satisfaction.

But to me alone falls the full responsibility for any failure to do justice to the subjects of this work. For surely in the lives of these women, there was more than enough material to work with.

With that said, as is the way of our African ancestors, I ask permission of the eldest of them to speak.

Lillian Belle Miles

Lil

It is only fitting that I begin with the first woman I knew—my mother, Lillian Belle Miles. "Lil," as everyone including her children called her, was born in 1915 to Billy and Josie Miles, both of whom were of mixed Native and African American ancestry, in a small town just across the North Carolina border in Virginia named Boykins. She was the last of eight children born of the union of her mother and her father. Lil's older brother Norman was born of a relationship between her father and another woman.

As I remember Boykins, fondly from childhood visits, it sat among pine trees, cotton fields, lumber mills, and a peanut factory. My grandfather was a small farmer, who raised chickens, pigs, collard greens, sweet potatoes, corn, tomatoes, and watermelons.

Cap'n Billy, as my grandfather was called respectfully by all who knew him outside of the family, had connections with all those enterprises through his mules and wagons, using them to haul logs to the sawmill, cotton to the gin, and peanuts to the factory.

Lil tells of being a sickly child from birth. One of her favorite stories was how, at a preschool age, her father wrapped her body first in leaves and then in blankets and kept the fire going in the wood-burning stove one cold Virginia night to sweat the whooping cough out of her. Throughout her life, Lil, a natural survivor, would not let her frail, small stature deter her from something once she set her mind to it.

This served her well, for although both of her parents could barely read, write, or cipher, they wanted more for Lillian and her siblings, sending Lil off to Norfolk to live with her brother William so that she could get a high school education. They willingly paid for her books and room and board. With the completion of school, she did not want to remain in Virginia. Lil went to Harlem, living with her married sister Ethel, and took a job as a nurse's aide.

At a weekend house party—which at the time, along with churches, bars, beauty parlors, barbershops, and dance halls, were central to Black social life—Lil met the man who was to be her first husband: John Washington Saunders. He was a brown-skinned handsome multitalented son of the Caribbean, having been born in Nevis, British West Indies.

John earned his living as a painter, carpenter, and roofer. He also played the guitar, made drums and flutes, and had a powerful tenor voice that could be heard above all others in Ebenezer Wesleyan Methodist Church, where he led the drum and bugle corps. Women loved him. They were drawn to him like bees to a hive, and he to them. (His love of women and their love of him would contribute to the breakup of his marriage and, eventually, to his death).

Lil and John were to have a tumultuous marriage. She, beautiful, vivacious, strong willed; he, a macho West Indian and just as strong willed. She was to admit in her later years that she married John as a way out of her sister's house. Why he married her, outside of the fact that, along with her other attributes, she was "high yaller," was never really clear. (It is hopeful to believe that perhaps in his own way he actually loved her as much as he could love any woman).

John and Lil lived in Bedford-Stuyvesant, Brooklyn, New York. They had three children, two boys—John Washington, the eldest, and myself—and a girl, Mildred Olivia. These children were born at two-year intervals. John had a daughter, Sylvia, by another woman in 1935, the same year my oldest brother, John, was born. Lil was to take Sylvia into her home at different times, maintaining a relationship with her throughout her developing years.

Their own children, John, Bernard, and Mildred, grew up in a home with the mixed culture of the Southern USA and the English-speaking Caribbean. Thus, we were exposed to fried chicken, potato salad, collard greens, turned corn meal, okra, salt fish, and callaloo.

My father's business thrived. He was able to open a small shop on Lewis Avenue in Bedford-Stuyvesant. The children attended PS 129 on Gates Avenue. The oldest girl, Sylvia, lived around the corner on Halsey Street with our grandmother, Sarah, her daughter, Clarissa, and her two sons, Charles and Tom, and Tom's daughter, Judy.

The bitterness engendered by this dual birth would affect family relationships for generations. Notwithstanding that strain, there was daily interaction between the two households.

Lil continued to work as a nurse's aide. John continued womanizing and drinking. Lil, perhaps propelled by her independence, wanted to attend a government-sponsored nursing school program during World War II.

John wanted no part of the government. An independent person to a fault, he never became a naturalized citizen of the United States. Turmoil became a permanent part of my parents' marriage as their wills clashed. They knew which buttons to push on one another. At times it led to violence.

When John fractured Lil's nose, she packed up her three children and, despite the restrictions on travel during World War II, transported us to Virginia to live with her parents. Lil completed nursing school and brought the children north again. The oldest (John) and the youngest (Mildred) were to join her at her brother Norman's apartment in the Bronx, New York. I was to live with my father and his common-law wife, Juanita Atkins. (I have fond memories of Juanita Atkins. She was a good-humored, brown-skinned earthy daughter of the South, who worked as a domestic. She treated John's children as if they were her own. To my knowledge, she had no children. That woman made the best fried chicken—bar none—that I have ever tasted. She loved my father dearly. I have lost track of her over the years, much to my regret.)

At fifteen years old, tired of my father's restrictions, even though I had my own room, I gave in to the need to join my mother and siblings living in the Bronx with Lil's brother Norman. I left my father's home. In Uncle Norman's spacious apartment, the four of us shared our sleeping space with a refrigerator.

During the time Lil was living in the Bronx, she had fallen in love with Sam Phillips. She and Sam had traveled in the same circles before, during, and after her marriage failed. He was extremely generous and kind to Lil and her children. Sam made the lightest, sweetest coffee I've ever tasted. When he died unexpectedly, Lil was distraught. Sam's death marked the beginning of Lil's relationship with Howard McGuire.

Howard was a longshoreman, pitch black, a sharp dresser, and a big bald man with a penchant for big new cars. Thought to be a Southerner, he spoke in a clipped precise manner, which gave little clue to his roots. Lil and Howard were to eventually purchase a house together in Corona Queens, New York. Lil moved her three children into that house, providing them with their first independent living quarters since the dissolution of her marriage to John. As children, the three of us were at odds with him throughout Howard and Lil's marriage.

More than anything else, I think now with the passage of time, our disagreements with Howard McGuire, besides his stern manner, were due more to our sense that Lil and Howard were not getting along with each other.

But from that secure base, we were to firm up the foundations that would serve us well for the remainder of her life and ours. I was to finish high school in 1956 while living there, eventually leaving for the army to return to the same house in 1960. By that time, my brother, John, who was in college when I left, had married and left; and my sister, Mildred, had moved to live her life independently.

Within two years of my own marriage in 1963, Lil's marriage to Howard was finished amidst acrimony about ownership of the property. It was years before it was settled.

The breakup of Lil's marriage to Howard set the stage for the second great love affair of Lil's life. Milton Collins was cut out of the same cloth as Sam Phillips. In fact, they may have known each other through Sam. Milton was a big soft-spoken brown man of the streets, who was nobody to fool with. When they met, Milton was assembling cars for General Motors in Tarrytown, New York. He loved the best in life. He drank the best liquor and purchased the best clothes. He was a gambler, dirt-track race driver, and a great lover of music, particularly jazz. Eventually his collection was to number hundreds of tapes, including reel to reels, 45s, and long-playing albums.

At the time they married, Milton was living in the upstairs apartment of a two-family home (owned by the Gettoes family, the in-laws of John, Lil's oldest son) in Hollis Queens. They were to live there happily for many years. During this same period, Lil nursed her older brother Norman in the Bronx, who was ill and legally blind (although he still managed to drive a car even though he was functionally illiterate) until he died at the age of ninety. She was also instrumental in burying John, the father of her three children.

It became evident overtime that Lil had asthma. Lil was forced to retire from her job as a licensed practical nurse in New York City-owned hospitals. In her words, she had "rode the bus" as an ambulance attendant nurse for twenty years. Her back had been injured in assisting a patient from a stretcher to a bed. She received a disability pension check for that. She continued working as a private-duty nurse until her age and illness forced her to stop.

For some reason not entirely clear to me, the situation between Lil and Milton became strained. They separated and finally divorced. Lil (as was her way) did not wait long before she entered into a relationship with Charles Merritt, who was a boilermaker by trade. They purchased a home together in Bayside, New York. Charles was short of stature and of temper, much like her first husband, John. Their marriage was doomed practically from the outset. He would not stomach her independence; she could not tolerate his bitterness. He also insisted on keeping dogs, which she felt he thought more of than her, especially with the onset of her asthma.

When that marriage failed, she called on Milton Collins, her third husband, for help. He made room once more in his life and apartment for her.

Milton left the car-assembly plant to return to work in the post office, the job he had left to enter the army in World War II. He reasoned that he could retire with his total federal time earlier, and that the plant was scheduled to be closed.

With her private-duty work as a nurse, her disability check, and a second-hand car Milton maintained for her (he never purchased new cars; he did not believe in them—he believed used cars had proven themselves), Lil had finally achieved the independence she had been striving for all her life.

The second time worked. They were to live happily together for years. Their own happiness was reinforced in many ways by the warm relationship they had with their grandchildren and Lil with her children.

The grandchildren believed that there was nothing they could not discuss with her, for they trusted her to honor their confidence. They knew she would listen. She would not judge them. She would offer sage advice when they wanted it. They loved her. And they were assured she loved them.

Lil always had one of her sky-blue checks for them on their birthdays. They knew she was good for it when their money was short. And they would pay her back when they could or she would ask them for it. They did not want it to come to that because they did not want the lecture on being accountable and responsible for debts that came with it.

As she aged, Lil's asthma became problematic. At one point, her doctors had her on experimental drugs. She would be hospitalized once or twice a year, for two or three days at a time, until her condition stabilized. Invariably, she would adopt or be adopted by a patient, staff member, doctor, nurse, aide, or a candy striper. She just accumulated people, sometimes much to the chagrin of her children. We would be there with her as much as the hospital rules allowed and beyond, depending on her condition, doing battle with successive administrators and managers in shifts to assure the quality of her care did not diminish.

The situation between Lil and Milton again became strained. We were to find out later that it was due in part to the beginning of his battle with cancer; when he moved out of their apartment, we had no idea what was going on. In one of life's more ironic twist, they began living in senior citizens' homes a short distance from one another, in Jamaica, Queens; in effect, they continued living together, for when you visited one, the other was there more often than not. As it became obvious that Milton was dying, they seemed to grow even closer together.

Lil never missed a beat. Always sustained by her unshakable belief in God, the sicker he got, the stronger she appeared. She organized the support needed to make his waning life comfortable. When he died, she arranged his funeral and his burial in the same plot with her brother Norman, where she herself would later be buried.

Under Lil's impetus and with the aid of her children, The Milton Collins Music Collection was established at the Schaumburg Center in Harlem, USA, as a permanent legacy of his love of music.

Lil went on. She was marvelously independent, helped by her car. She reveled in being able to drive at this late stage in her life. The car enabled her to do volunteer work and keep her commitments to her church. A lifelong Baptist, she loved working with children and taught generations in Sunday school. However, an unfortunate minor accident was to put a crimp in her independence.

After visiting her daughter, Mildred, one sunny afternoon, an elderly woman stepped off the curb against the light and walked into the side of Lil's slow-moving vehicle at a busy intersection in Flushing, Queens. She fell down, traumatizing both of them. Although it was eventually established that Lil was not at fault and there were no serious injuries, she began to curtail her driving, limiting herself to short trips under optimum conditions.

Her family filled the gap when she stopped driving altogether, but that did not sit well with her. As she aged, one of her central themes was that she never wanted to be a burden to her children.

Lil was not ready to give up just yet. She was floor captain in her seniors' complex, served as a volunteer in the dining room, and cooked and shared meals on her floor for those who could no longer do so for themselves.

An inveterate reader over the years, she began to pursue the history of Africa and its Diaspora, with books from the well-stocked shelves of her children. Lil also kept up a steady correspondence with a range of people. She began writing poetry, putting her innermost thoughts, long unexpressed, at least to her children, on paper. An aficionado of Black talk radio, she scanned the dials for diverse opinions, often well into dawn, thus allowing her to converse on a wide range of subjects. This was augmented by her extensive travels around the United States and abroad. She met and became a favorite of her first husband's, John, family in Antigua-Barbuda.

The asthma attacks increased and began to take their toll. Time between trips to the emergency room shortened, and hospital stays lengthened. Her apartment began to resemble a hospital room with the apparatus she needed to assist her breathing. Lil's conversation increasingly turned to the subject of her death. She had no fear of it, approaching it calmly as inevitable and, thus, to be planned, to be prepared for.

Each of her children in their individual visits would receive parts of her thoughts on the subject. We would share the information with each other. We also received detailed written instructions to supplement the verbal. Lil had insurance policies that covered her long-term care, filled the gaps in Medicare and Medicaid, and provided for continued income during her hospital stays.

She also had a living will, which stated she did not want to be kept alive by artificial means and wanted to receive only medications that would allow her to die peacefully and with as little pain as possible.

She was to die on February 6, 1993. Even here, she did it her way. Admitted to the emergency room for treatment after a series of severe attacks, her children were engaging the personnel on duty in their usual frontal attack on her behalf. When I leaned over to tell her that she was going to make it through this one, her eyes flashed with what I took to be anger. It haunted me for years until I concluded that she had decided that it was time to go and would brook no interference from anyone.

As she was in life, so she was in death. After death, she continued to exert her will. Not unexpectedly, her instructions for her funeral were detailed: the minister who was to officiate, the hymns to be sung, the color of the dress she would wear, the funeral director, her prepaid coffin, and grave opening fees were all accounted for.

Her legacy can be seen in the influence Lil's life continues to have on the lives of her children, grandchildren, and great-grandchildren. There is rarely a family gathering in which she is not a part of the discussion.

Thanks, Lil.

Charshee Lawrence McIntire

Charshee Charlotte Lawrence McIntyre

For me to write of Charshee is to set the standard for *Ordinary Women, Extraordinary Lives*. This, then, is admittedly a totally subjective personal homage to Charshee Charlotte Lawrence McIntyre. For this was the nature of my relationship to Charshee, as she was universally known. I was not alone; it was the same for so many who came in contact with her. That was one of Charshee's many endearing gifts—the ability to make you think, feel, and know an intimacy with her. I did not know this when I first met her in 1985.

I had recently dropped out of the doctoral program in political science at the City University of New York Graduate Center. A friend of mine from the program, Jennifer Squires (a woman of formidable intellect in her own right and a younger inheritor of the tenets of the subjects profiled in this book), told me that there was a class on African history being taught at Hunter by John Henrick Clarke that she monitored from time to time, which she thought I might be interested in.

That proved to be a turning point in my studies and my life.

Through Dr. Clarke and Dr. W. Ofuatey-Kodjoe, one of my professors at the Graduate Center, I was introduced to the African Heritage Studies Association (AHSA). At the time, Dr. Kodjoe was president of AHSA; he was organizing its annual conference. I volunteered to work with him and a group of students at Queens College to get it done. This largely involved stuffing envelopes for the mailings it takes to pull a conference of that magnitude together. It was through that effort that I met Charshee. She was on the executive board of AHSA.

My relationship with Charshee was largely a reflection of my relationship to AHSA. It was impossible to know Charshee and not know how dedicated she was to the Pan-African philosophy and the African-centered paradigm AHSA was founded to promote. It did not matter if you were a scholar, activist, or student. If you came within Charshee's orbit, you soon realized how committed she was to the worldwide struggle for the liberation of African people.

(Charshee's involvement in the struggle would grow to encompass Native American people and indigenous people worldwide as her knowledge of her own Native American roots—something we shared—in Nova Scotia grew. This would, at times, bring her into conflict with some of her more dogmatic African-centered colleagues in the movement. Of course, that did not deter Charshee from pursuing her ideas. She was not one to shy away from conflict or challenges to what she believed in).

After presenting a paper at that first conference on the African roots of Christianity, largely through Dr. Clarke's encouragement, it was easy for me to become involved in organizing the following one, which was to be Dr. Kodjoe's last as president of AHSA. In the intervening year, during numerous organizing meetings, we began to focus on Ofuatey's successor. The choice soon was narrowed to Charshee. For some reason, it fell upon me to convince her to accept nomination at the head of a slate that would assure the continuity of AHSA.

Charshee was a logical choice. She had been involved with AHSA for years and knew the major players. Because of this, it was not an easy sell. Charshee was all too familiar with the internal politics of the organization. She had also founded the Language Arts Department at the Westbury Campus of SUNY, while her husband, Ken Makanda McIntyre, headed the Music Department at the same campus; thus, she had more than a working knowledge of the formidable forces arrayed in opposition to AHSA's goals and objectives in academia.

After lengthy discussions that I am sure involved many of the stellar people nationally and internationally whom Charshee knew, she accepted. As part of the deal, I was to be her membership secretary. Thus began our working relationship. For four years, with Charshee leading the way and shouldering the bulk of the workload, we worked at AHSA practically full time.

Much of the work took place in the kitchen of her west Riverside Drive apartment in Manhattan, over one of Charshee's deliciously prepared plates of fried chicken. It was primarily through her will that new life and spirit was breathed into the AHSA.

But such was the way of Charshee Charlotte Lawrence McIntyre. She was born of African American / Native American ancestry in Boston on May 14, 1937; she joined the air force in 1950. Encouraged by her husband, Ken Makanda McIntyre, she went back to school in her thirties when she already had two children and attained two masters degrees and a Ph.D (Naya Arinde, *Daily Challenge*, May 24, 1999, 3.).

Throughout this remarkable journey, Charshee battled a series of health challenges: lupus, heart disease, and shingles. Blessed with an indomitable spirit, for years she was squired through life by her husband of forty-one years—Makanda, a remarkable human being in his own right.

Charshee loved to tell the story of how it was her beloved husband who insisted that she return to school at a time she was content to remain at home as the wife of a world-class musician while she raised her two sons, Kayjee and Khyle. Invariably, she would tell all that she had succeeded perfectly.

She also succeeded in making me and countless others believe that we were part of her great extended family. That was part of her genius. That was what she brought to me. As we sat in her kitchen or spoke during our ritual Monday-morning phone conversations, often while she was in the bathtub as part of her self-therapy for the health challenges she faced over the years, Charshee challenged my intellect, honed my mind, and reinforced my spirit.

Those conversations ranged well beyond the day-to-day business of implementing AHSA missions to encompass a wide range of subjects—spirituality, sexuality, and the link between them; a staunch supporter of the Black man, Charshee took issue to the negative image of the Black male portrayed by some of her contemporaries, although she did not suffer male chauvinism kindly.

Even as her illnesses began to take their toll, she continued to fight the battle to bring the rightful place of Africans on the continent, in the Diaspora, and Native Americans in history to the fore.

It was in no small part. Charshee's sojourn through the duality of her African and Native American heritage that I too was able to understand, to bridge my own tripartite: African-American, African-Caribbean, Native American heritage. It is among the many things that I will be eternally grateful to her for. It was a healing spiritual process for both of us. For as strong as Charshee's intellectual development was, it was matched by her spiritual evolution.

And it was here in the spirit of ancient Egypt's Maat—balance, justice, truth—that Charshee's multiculturalism came alive and set an example for those of us who desired to emulate her. Beloved as "Mama Charshee"—"Warrior Queen" to the army she helped to create across generations—the mandate is to continue the liberation struggle.

Spirituality, Pan-Africanism, African-centered, multiculturalism were not mere words to Charshee Charlotte Lawrence McIntyre. They were a way of life; they were also weapons, tools, and guideposts to be employed by those she bequeathed them to following her death, to be used to assure that her people—all of her people—understand and reclaim their place in history.

Following her death, Charshee's funeral actually was a celebration of her life. As Native American Asebe Tubahachi is quoted in the *Amsterdam News*, "She was of my blood and we must maintain our ownership of her, her sanctity . . ." (May 27-June 2, 1999).

With her transition, Charshee joined the ranks of women warriors who preceded her to the land of the ancestors, such as Nzinga, Sojourner Truth, Harriet Tubman, Rosa Parks, and Shirley Chisholm.

She will be right at home in such honored company.

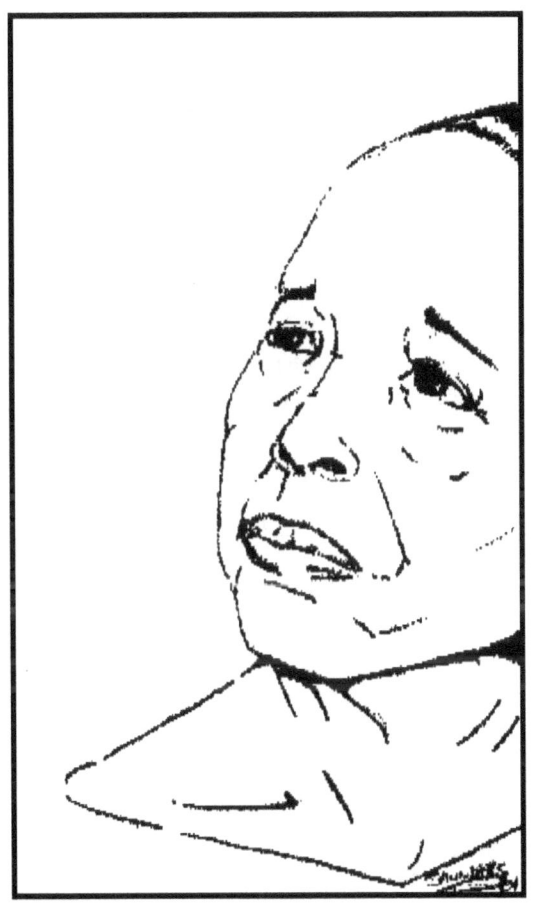

Marjorie Ransom

Marjorie Ransom

Warriors come in all stripes. I met Marjorie Ransom, a warrior in her own right, in the summer of 1994. She was the director of volunteers for the Museum for African Art (MAA) on Broadway, south of Houston (SoHo), in lower Manhattan. In her official volunteer capacity, she was responsible for recruiting and training volunteers for the museum's education department. Like everyone else who came into contact with Marjorie Ransom, I soon learned that her unofficial duties far exceeded the confines of her title.

I had been hired as a part-time security guard in July. That in itself was indicative of what I came to expect at the museum, although I had no way of knowing it at the time. I had come to see the museum's Secrecy exhibition and was impressed. So much so that I made a casual remark to the guard at the front door as I entered that I had always wanted to work in a place like that as I looked around the museum store.

He told me to stop by and see him on the way out if I was serious. By the time I returned, I was enthralled not only by the exhibition but also by the museum itself. I said as much to the guard. He told me to contact a Kathy McAuliffe, who was deputy director, and gave me her phone number. He also said that he expected there would be vacancies in the security department in the near future.

I did not know at the time that I was talking to Bart Roussevere, the chief of security. I went home that evening and wrote Ms. McAuliffe, detailing my years of experience in the security field, including my twenty years with the New York City Department of Correction. Shortly afterward, I was interviewed and hired. I could not believe my good fortune. I was actually going to get paid to work in an institution that would allow me to further my studies into my culture. I worked as a part-timer over the Fourth of July weekend.

My part-time employment was short-lived. Bart Rousevere was planning on leaving in a matter of weeks. I was offered his job, and I accepted. The full-time security staff consisted of two other guards (Lear Riojas and Kwabena Antwi of Ghana) and a maintenance person (Debbie Whitfield), who doubled as security when needed. The staff was augmented by part-timers and contract guards on a need basis.

From the outset, Ms. Ransom, a consummate museum professional based on her thirty years of experience, much of it at the Museum of Natural History, became a guiding light for me. I had never worked in a museum before. I came to rely on her counsel as just about everyone else in the museum, for Marjorie Ransom was a remarkable combination of intelligence, sophistication, experience, and sensitivity. An active listener, she could converse on a universe of subjects.

When I think of Ms. Majorie Ransom, I envision a lady. For that is what she was in every sense of the word. In her tweeds, she dressed like one, spoke like one, and carried herself like one. Given my generation, she was Lena Horne, Dorothy Dandridge, and Katharine Hepburn.

On more than one occasion, Marjorie was able to diffuse tension with her wisdom. This was especially true for me. The longer I stayed at the museum, the more the bloom faded. Often my security instincts were in conflict with other units of the museum and the museum's ever present financial perils. Also, my African-centered, Pan-African perspective brought me into conflict with the museum's Euro-centered view of Africa and its culture.

Marjorie's level of dedication to the museum bordered on legendary. In the four years that I worked with her, she rarely missed a day, most of the time being one of the first ones in and the last to leave, often seven days a week.

This was especially true when the education department was planning training for volunteers around a specific exhibition, running tour groups, or assisting in staging special events—a source of much-needed income for the museum.

Marjorie liked to get in early, have her coffee, and read the *New York Times*. Her early arrival also gave schools calling in to plan field trips to the museum someone to talk to. This was important to Marjorie. She wanted to be in a position to accommodate teachers, many of whom she had trained over the years she had worked in museums.

This also afforded the other early arrivals at MAA the opportunity to sit around and talk to Ms. Ransom before the Museum geared up for its full workday. It was during those sessions and other times when Marjorie was in the art galleries that my image of her was formed. It was an image she generated.

Ms. Ransom's image of herself was reinforced by her presence. She was a diminutive woman of about five feet in height. She weighed about one hundred pounds. Her salt-and-pepper hair was worn pulled back in a bun, exposing her olive complexion, oval face, high cheekbones, aquiline nose, hazel eyes, and perked lips.

Marjorie said she was the only child of her parents and was raised in a nonreligious environment to be an independent thinker. Because they did not want her to be dependent on any particular philosophy or creed, she was exposed to the great thinkers of the Western world at an early age.

Ms. Ransom always spoke standard English. In my day, it would have been called speaking proper. She was always poised, and I cannot remember seeing her angry. That does not, however, mean she was not capable of anger; she just chose not to express it in an overt emotional manner. Her approach was in keeping with her persona.

One of her favorite tales dealt with being approached by a European woman in a five-star hotel in Paris, who inquired if Marjorie was seeking employment as a maid. Ms. Ransom's response was telling.

The flash in Marjorie's intelligent eyes as she told the story many years later demonstrated a residue of strong emotions, if not anger. Ms. Ransom stated that as she stood there in her Chanel suit with matching accessories, she looked her questioner in the eye and replied calmly that she would ask her own maid if she knew of anyone looking for work. The stunned European had nothing else to say to Ms Ransom.

That incident exemplifies Marjorie's approach to prejudice in issues of race, class, and gender. She did not deny the existence of biases—she chose to live her life in such a way to minimize its effect on her. Majorie said she and her retired engineer husband lived in a cooperative apartment on seventy-some odd street on the west side of Manhattan. Their daughter was a surgeon. Marjorie spent a part of every summer on their horse farm in Pennsylvania.

At one point, Marjorie caused consternation on the part of a woman of European extraction regarding the horses. It was as if, Marjorie said with a chuckle, that she could not bring herself to believe that "we could own horses." Humor, sometimes risqué, was part of the arsenal that Ms. Ransom was quite adept at employing on a need basis, dictated by the circumstances.

Ms. Ransom professed not to be particularly drawn to African art or culture nor did she believe herself to be religious or spiritual. Yet in her consummate humanity, she lived by many of the values not only inherent in African culture but also those purported to be the basis of the major Western religions—Judaism, Christianity, Islam—and demonstrated spirituality in interacting with others, which many persons I have known, who professed to be both religious and spiritual, did not.

Whatever Marjorie's belief system, there was no question that she was a teacher. She taught would-be teachers, teachers, and students. She taught me the museum business from the inside. She taught museum managers. She taught children—although here again, she claimed she was not enamored of them.

But all you had to do was see her hold tykes enthralled during their museum visits or critique a docent's (museum volunteer) presentation to a group of visitors to understand her commitment to teaching. Her commitment to education was, in part, what fueled her longevity at MAA. She was well aware of the museum's shortcomings. Nonetheless, Marjorie believed that it was an invaluable teaching tool and, as such, that her presence there made a difference in implementing the institution's alleged educational mission.

Ms. Ransom was the education department of MAA, no matter who the titular director was during my four-year tenure.

Marjorie's influence on me was such that we stayed in touch with each other after I left MAA. We would meet for lunch at one of her favorite Italian bistros in SoHo or for dinner after work in a take-out place across the street from the MAA. She was just as comfortable in either one, just as she was at peace with museum directors or bus drivers. The bus drivers on the route she took between the museum and her home on the west side knew her well and spoke to her, and of her, with obvious affection.

It was during these meetings after I was no longer employed at MAA that I began to discuss my idea for including her in this work. I became aware that her health was deteriorating during the few times that we were able to meet.

Life intervened, and I was never able to sit down with her with my tape recorder as I have done with the other subjects portrayed here. But even as she became increasingly frail, she never stopped doing for others.

In death, she continued to define herself. She died alone but was not destitute. No husband. No daughter. Her death added to the mystique, the mystery of her life.

Yet anyone attending her funeral at the funeral home on her beloved west side of Manhattan or later at the memorial for her at the Museum for Natural History knows just how large, multidimensional, multiethnic, multicultural, and multiracial this extraordinary woman's family was. For humanity was clearly her family.

In the life of Marjorie Ransom, there are lessons for all of us who survive her.

Sarah Sally Buntin Payne

Sarah Buntin Payne

The life of Sarah Buntin Payne was a journey of an ever-evolving spirit into a rock-solid faith. She was born January 3, 1920, in the village of Salem on the volcanic island of Montserrat, a British colony in the leeward islands of the Caribbean. Sarah was left by her mother with her paternal grandmother, Hannah Fenton Buntin, when she was three months old.

Her small frame, frail and bent by age, Sarah recalled a happy childhood. Both her grandmother and great-great-grandmother, who Sarah remembers as a very old woman, were women of the church. Therefore, Sarah says, "I got to know the Lord early." Blessed with "studyation," according to Sarah, instead of education, her grandmother had a profound effect on the woman Sarah matured into.

Hannah Fenton Buntin was a laborer on the Montserrat Company estates, owned by a family from England. The most substantial crop on the island at the time was cotton, although limes were also grown. The cottons seeds were turned into cooking oil and black soap, while the juice was extracted from the limes. During holidays (birthday of the British monarch or other British holidays) from school, Sarah would accompany her grandmother during cotton-picking time. By law, children could not work the fields when school was in session.

The cotton was planted by teams of men, women, and children. The women would clear the grass that had grown since the field was last harvested. The men formed banks of earth into which cottonseeds were planted by children—two to each hole in the bank made by poking the earth with a stick. Once the plants reached two inches in height, they were weeded for two months. Flowers bloomed on the stems first, followed by white cotton balls.

Adults were paid one penny (2 US cents) for every four pounds of cotton picked. But it had to be trashed and cleaned before it was weighed. They went to the fields at eight in the morning and worked until dark. The field had to be picked three times a week. Payday was always on Fridays. After the fields were picked clean, children were hired to uproot the plants; what remained was burned to prevent pink worm, which was devastating to cotton crops. The children were paid eight to twelve cents a day.

Like most Montserratians, Sarah's grandmother owned her own clapboard, thatched-roof, two-room house and a small plot of land that she cultivated or farmed. Ownership was determined by ancestry, with some people having to rent. To have animals graze on the plantation, you had to be employed at least as a laborer there.

There was no electricity or indoor plumbing available to the vast majority of the people of Montserrat. When it was dry, cooking was done outside on an iron coal pot set over three stones. Some of the more fortunate would have a shed, where the cooking was done when it rained. The embers left over after cooking were used to iron clothes.

The ironing was done with a "Grey Goose," so-called because its iron body resembled a fowl (Jane, has her mother's with her). There was a second smaller iron; it was heated on the top of the stove (we have that one with us also).

Clothing was washed in Belham River by standing in the water and rubbing the clothes against a flat rock with a dry cornhusk. The river, at that time, the largest on the island, had an abundance of lobsters, mullet, and eel. Children would collect water from the river or the village standpipe and wood from the forest to take home for cooking, often balancing the loads on their heads.

The river is dry now. When the Europeans decided they wanted water in their houses, this river and others were dammed to provide the water required for their indoor toilets and kitchens.

Jane still gets angry when she discusses the loss of her beloved river. To her it is one more example of the injustices the inhabitants of the villages were subjected to at the hands of the Europeans.

Children walked to school. Sarah started at five years of age. School was compulsory and public school was free. Before being admitted, the children had to line up daily for their feet, hands, nails, teeth, and hair to be examined for cleanliness. (Jane underwent the same inspections when she attended school on the island.)

All children learned geography, arithmetic, and general knowledge. Girls were taught sewing and housekeeping; boys, science and gardening. In general the teachers were from the Caribbean, traveling between the Leeward Islands to pursue their profession.

These were good times for Sarah. She says, "I would walk to town on Saturday with the rest of the schoolchildren to shop. I would stop at the Botanical gardens that had benches to sit on and admire the wild flowers, the water lilies, roses of all colors, yellow alamanders, and white lilies that could be smelled from afar."

At the market, thick sticky black sugar was purchased by the gallon, flour by the bag. Some of it was stored for future use; some would be shared with the less fortunate. Children being children, some of them pilfered black sugar for their own use. One of those times when Sarah, in her righteousness, admonished the children for this, she was severely beaten by them. This brought adults in the village to Sarah's defense.

Montserrat, she continued, "was a bountiful land with mangos, cashews, green and red plums," which is one reason she believes so many expatriates from Europe and the United States made it home, despite severe hurricanes in 1924 and 1928 and an earthquake in 1935. She had also seen more than one volcanic eruption in her lifetime.

(It was so green that it was known as the Emerald Isle of the Caribbean. This, too, is a hallmark of the Irish-indentured servants, who were brought to Montserrat by the colonizing British to act as overseers of the plantations when enslaved Africans were the main source of labor. Slavery officially ended on Montserrat in 1834. There remains a strong connection between Montserrat and Ireland, with many Montserratians celebrating St. Patrick's Day).

Sarah, like many Montserratians of her generation, knew that hurricanes are seasonal, with the high wind and raw rain. They knew that when the weatherglass was down, they must look south to check conditions and start boarding up the houses. Churches and schools were used then, as now, as hurricane shelters for those who did not have secure quarters in their houses.

"Life is short," she says. "In those short days, a lot of things happen." That included earthquakes and hurricanes. Sarah considered such events as part of the ups and downs of life.

Whatever happened, Sarah learned, her resourceful grandmother apparently had a solution for it—one more reason Sarah believes that "intelligence does not mean education," for her grandmother was a "grandmother to every child in the village." She would work leeches to relieve bad blood; use syringes filled with compounds made from roots and herbs for other ailments; make certain teas for women to use for birth control; and pound white-headed flowers into juice, add salt, and administer it for belly gripe. Sarah's face contorts when she states, "It tastes bad. I would rather feel the pain than take the medicine, senna, and salt for being cleaned out before the start of each school term. The ancestors left this . . ."

(That too was in effect when Jane went to school. She uses it now.)

Christmas was a special time for children. Despite subsistent living, every effort was made to provide them with dainties, like cake, cassava bread, candies, and confections made from sweet potato, guava, and coconut.

Sarah herself completed ordinary school; she did not attend secondary standard. After leaving school, Sarah supported herself by picking cotton, helping her grandmother with sewing, crochet, and handcrafts that were sold to other people. She first left Montserrat as a teenager, traveling to Dominica. It was there, when visiting her aunt Tantan at the age of seventeen, that she met the man who would be her husband—Fred Payne.

Although born on Montserrat, he was working in Dominica at the time. They would marry in December 1939, when she was twenty years old; and began to cultivate their own land. Sarah taught local girls handcrafts and dressmaking. Their first child was to be born one year later. Like many men of his time, Fred would follow work where it led him.

He cut sugarcane in Florida, spent two years in England working in the foundries, and served in the British army in Antigua. He eventually became a renowned forest ranger, consulted for his knowledge of the flora of the island.

Sarah states that when the men were overseas, the families would meet the steamer bringing letters and packages at the dock. During this time, "some will cry," she said, "and some would laugh," depending on if they received something or not.

One year before Sarah left Montserrat for the first time, on Easter Sunday, at the age of sixteen, she was received as a full member of the Salem Wesleyan Methodist Church. She said she shed "tears of joy" at the time.

The pastor, Reverend Lawrence from England, recommended Sarah to be the leader of her Sunday-school class. The church was separated into age groups, and because of this, Sarah's nomination met with some opposition because of her youth. The minister persisted, saying, "Eventually they will come to you." He was right; Sarah had to "turn another page" in her Sunday-school attendance ledger, as her class became the largest in the church.

Sarah would go on to became the first "local" woman lay Methodist preacher (not ordained) on Montserrat, often preaching at other denominations. At first apprehensive, she "asked the Lord to be her teacher," reasoning " . . . never say no to the Lord." She also became the Women's League president.

She marks the birth of her children by the ministers who baptized them: Reverend Lawrence would baptize her first three children, Edna, Richard, and Kenneth, before he returned to England; Mary Rose and Theodora were baptized by Reverend Hillard; the last of her children, Jane, was baptized by Reverend Thomas.

It was at the time of the birth of her daughter Theodora that Sarah got to know her own mother, who had raised another family in St. Thomas. Sarah bares her no ill will.

In fact, this woman appeared incapable of bearing ill will toward anyone. While growing up, she even sympathized with the fictitious characters she read about in such books as *Jane Eyre* and *Snow White*, initially thinking they were real and then learning that "they have lessons," such as the mirror and the poisoned apple.

Her husband, Fred Payne, would tell her that "she sympathized too deeply . . . ," admonishing her for "taking on other people's problems when she had her own children to raise."

Nonetheless, like her grandmother, she felt all the children in the village were hers; when sewing for her children, she would sew for others as well.

Sarah said, "By thoughts, words, or the sharing of simple gifts . . . whatever little things were in the house I would make into packets and send to people with children."

Growing up in the church as she did, people felt safe in sharing their confidences with her; she would say, "If I am going to tell anyone, I would let you know. It is not my business to tell anyone."

Sarah believes that being a Christian does not rule out spirit. "Ancestors, [as well] as good friends . . . are present with you [after death] . . . return in spirit, dreams, feelings, to guide us . . ." In fact, Sarah believes that her beloved friend Nenzie "passed the torch of wisdom to her" on her deathbed as she held Nenzie's hand, and it cracked in hers during her transition from the realm of the living into that of the ancestors.

(This belief of Sarah, if widely known, would have put her at odds with many of her peers although it is aligned with the aforementioned African traditions.)

(At the time of death, another ancestral ritual with strong African roots would be activated; the body of the deceased would be washed and dressed by women of the village. The big toes would be tied together and the jaw tied with a cloth, the knot being made at the top of the head. A shroud would be placed on the body. An all-night wake would be held, hymns sung, and prayers recited; wreaths were made and then a funeral would be held in the local church with the burial in cemeteries, usually by denomination. Far be it for a person from one denomination to be buried in the cemetery or another; or for one race to be buried in the cemetery of another—people were separated in death as they were in life.

(One of the more notable observations I have made about Montserrat are the number of Christian denominations on the island. Given the small size of the island's population [thirteen thousand at its pre-volcanic eruption peak], the large number of denominations bears witness to Christianity's competition to influence the life of the islanders.)

(The presence of all of these churches has failed to eradicate the practice of religious/spiritual practices indigenous to Africa. These spiritual traditions—known variously as obeah, juju, and voodoo—came to the islands with enslaved Africans. It remains rooted in their descendants despite centuries of efforts to stamp it out.)

Speaking cautiously but with great conviction, she said, "Faith has great meaning." She continued, "Some people take it as religion, but it is more than that. Trust in the Lord; there can be no meaningful religion without faith and spirit . . ."

"In seventy-five years," Sarah stated, "there are a lot of things that cannot be remembered . . ."

She did remember thinking, like so many of her time, that America was too far to visit. But she did so in 1979, returning twice after that. The last visit was caused by the eruption of the La Soufriere volcano. She, like many others, left the island when conditions became intolerable. But after a lengthy stay in the United States and over the protest of her children, she decided to return home to her beloved island. She longed for her flower gardens and the warmth of the people of her village. She had found the climate and the people of the United States "too cold" for her liking.

It seems to me, someone who has been privileged to have known her since I married her daughter, Jane, that she has forgotten more than most of us have learned about living and still knew a lot that many of us ought to know.

Sarah Sally Buntin Payne made her transition to the realm of the ancestors on November 22, 2007. She was laid to rest next to her beloved husband, Fred Payne, in the cemetery of Salem Wesleyan Methodist Church.

Sybil Williams Clarke

Sybil Williams Clarke

Midway into the tapings, which were sprinkled with humor and laced with the molten spirit that form the basis of this profile of Sybil Williams Clarke, she quotes her mother with obvious pride as saying, in one of their discussions on religion when Sybil was a young girl in Jamaica, West Indies, "If you live up to the canon, do unto others as you would have them do unto you then you do not have to be concerned about a particular religion."

This became Sybil's creed. "That is why," Sybil said with soft-spoken passion, "that I extend myself to others."

At the time of the interviews, Sybil Williams Clarke was a seventy-five-year-old activist living in Harlem, USA. She was born in Jamaica on June 21, 1923. Thus, she, too, grew up under the British colonial system. Jamaica was a crown colony. Under this system of governing, all major decisions for the island were made in London.

Her mother was a housewife, her father, a "master cabinet maker." Sybil was one of thirteen children born into the household. Sybil's father, the son of a landowner who owned ninety acres and raised horses (family lore has it that he was poisoned with ground glass), worked seven days a week to support his family, making furniture for Jamaica's middle and upper class.

Sybil describes her father with obvious pride as a proud, independent man not one to take guff from anybody. He had left his secure employment with a large firm, because he did not like the way they were treating him. She remembers that he was a caring, giving man. No one who ever came to their home in need of a meal was ever denied a seat at their table.

Sybil was to inherit her father's pride, independence, and compassion.

Sybil attended an Anglican school up to the sixth grade; she then went to a technical school to study typing and bookkeeping. She would finish courses at a private school to become a secretary. While in public school,

Sybil would often eat lunch with her paternal Jewish grandmother, who sold food from a cart in order to support herself.

Her grandmother, who never married, eventually became so successful that she hired others to assist her in the preparation of the food she sold at the beach and in town. At the end of her workday, the grandmother would give away whatever food she had left over to the less fortunate.

Always inquisitive, never shy, Sybil once asked her grandmother how she could make money giving the food away; taking Sybil to where the water met the beach, the grandmother pointed to the waves, saying with humility, "You see the water returning to the beach? What I am doing is casting my bread upon the water. If it does not return to me, it will someday return to you."

That lesson became an integral part of Sybil's life.

Sybil grew up in what she characterizes as an extended family system. (At thirteen years of age, Sybil had met her first African, a seaman from Ghana who had escorted her blind brother home during World War II. The Ghanaian had explained the African extended family system to her as the reason for his concern about her brother, another Black man. Sybil immediately saw the similarity between what he said and how she lived).

She was to learn the extended family (in Jamaica, the Caribbean, and North America among persons of African ascent) was a holdover from slavery, as were people living together without the benefit of marriage. She said "a standard for a quality of living for human dignity that included the poor was established," in her family, "[which] was more or less the norm in Jamaica and throughout the Caribbean, for all we had was each other."

Within that context, Sybil continues to ask quietly to this day as is her rote, but with noticeable passion, as is her spirit, "If we do not help each other, who will?"

Sybil states that this extended family system was corrupted by class and a "caste of color" from "dark to light." Her own complexion burnished to copper tones by the sun, her hair bronzed by it; she said with clear distaste, although with a chuckle, the caste system existed in her own family, and still exists in Jamaica, and the United States among persons of African descent.

According to Sybil, neither of her parents were political activists. Although the fact that they, at one time, owned the only radio in the immediate area, made their home a gathering place for the community, where people would come to "listen to Joe Louis fight."

That politically related discussions followed such community social events was seen as part of the natural order of things. There are fewer things Caribbean people enjoy more than avidly, often than not, heated discussions of politics.

Activism, Sybil states with relish, is well-grounded in the Jamaican experience. Enslaved Africans took to the hills to fight against the cruelty of the British enslavers, forming three Maroon communities and burning many plantations in the process. Emancipation was won by enslaved Africans in Jamaica in 1838.

The Maroons were not the only derivatives of the enslaved Africans that Sybil Williams was familiar with. As a child, she had viewed Pocomania, a Yoruba-rooted religious derivative (from what is now modern Nigeria), that she was not allowed to delve into because Christianity disapproved of it. (Sybil's father, a bible-quoting "agnostic," never believed in "the white man's god.")

Sybil witnessed the continuation of this activism under the leadership of men, such as Michael Manley and his National Party,

Alexander Bustamante of the Labor Party, and William Grant, a leading Garveyite. These men led a march in Kingston, demanding self-government.

The goal of self-government was achieved in 1960, when Jamaica became independent.

(It was during the transformation to power for Jamaicans that another African derivative, the Rastafarians—users of the "spiritual weed," ganja and worshippers of Emperor Haile Selassie of Ethiopia, the Lion of Judah—gained prominence. Michael Manley, future prime minister of Jamaica engaged them in dialogue, and people, such as the noted writer Louise Bennett, recognized their talent and way of life, inviting them into her home).

The advent of Jamaican independence found Sybil Williams in the United States, having immigrated in 1947 at the age of twenty-five. In the United States of 1947, one could not get a government job unless you were a US citizen, so Sybil, who had worked as a legal secretary in Jamaica, went to work in a garment factory.

She immediately joined the union, the ILGWU, under which she took refresher courses in business. This led to a job with some Black lawyers on 125th Street in Harlem that, in turn, led to a job with a Black publisher's representative.

In 1957, Sybil Williams states that she took a job with the national office of the NAACP. She would remain with them for nine and a half years. She started with the youth division, helping to organize some of the first student sit-ins of the civil rights movement. During her tenure, forty young people from east Africa were brought into the USA for a dinner at the Waldorf Astoria.

Also, Medgar Evers, the murdered civil rights leader, attended a meeting just before he was killed. Sybil states that he knew he was going to be killed because of his work.

Again, her pride is evident when she says there were 1,700 branches before she left the NAACP due to policy differences, each with a youth division that participated in the March on Washington.

While with the NAACP, Sybil had given birth to a physically challenged daughter, who died in 1971. Sybil's father died in 1958, her mother in 1986 at ninety-nine years of age. Sybil provided for all of them while they lived.

Through such mechanisms as the *sou-sou*, which she states with a certainty that is so much a part of her personality, an African system of saving money, she and others put young members of her family through college.

The *sou-sou* is a system under which each person in a group contributes a set amount of money regularly to a fund for a given period of time. At the end of that time, one person gets the entire fund. It continues until each participant has gotten a "hand" or received the entire fund.

Sybil stated with conviction, " . . . money is to provide for that which humans need . . . not only yourself but others. Family, friends . . . the *sou-sou* is a traditional African way of doing things . . . spread the money around . . . it is based on trust . . . it comes back to you . . ."

Being her father's daughter, not being able to take guff from anyone was ingrained in her physic, so not withstanding her continued responsibilities, Sybil left the NAACP abruptly, without any job prospects. She states, with her Jamaican roots still audible in her voice, "I have to believe in me—that I can do what I have to do."

Through a former colleague, who had heard she had left the NAACP, Sybil Williams attained a job as an administrative assistant in the Department of Poverty during the administration of Mayor John Lindsey. She says that that agency had some of the best Black minds in the city employed there at the time, people like John Edmonds, Bruce Wright, and Carl McCall.

Its mandate was to provide services to the underserved, using federal money, in such areas as education, job training, social skills, theater and the arts. The program evolved into Model Cities and then was folded into the General Services Administration. Among its other successes, during Sybil's tenure, was the development of a database of first central Harlem and then all other city-held housing, which were formerly privately owned.

For example at one time, the city owned 65 percent of the housing in central Harlem. Under the Koch administration, this database was turned over to two colleges and universities in the city.

Sybil Williams would retire from the Department of General Services in 1986.

During that time, her "activism"—as John Henrik Clarke would later describe—her activities, and her support of her family had not slackened. She became familiar with the writing of 19th century Pan-Africanists, such as Wilmot Blyden and Martin Delaney. Her interest in Garvey never waned. She had also started attending First World lectures in 1982/1983, at which such leading African world thinkers as John Henrik Clarke, Josef Ben Jochommon (Dr. Ben), Asa Hillard, and a host of others, such as Jake Carruthers, Francis Cress Welsing, and Charshee McIntyre came to speak on Saturday afternoons in Harlem. In 1983/1984, she traveled with Dr. Ben to Egypt.

Here, we get to the heart of the beliefs that motivates Sybil Williams, when she passionately stated, " . . . self-help has to be an ethic, a human value, a way of life . . . it is what you do with the value of the human spirit . . . in life there are givers and takers . . . it's simple. The givers come back—the majority of people in the Diaspora are givers . . . the takers are corrupted . . ."

In listening to Sybil Williams Clarke, it is evident that she has a clear understanding of the relationship between religion, money, and power and the differences between the views of people with an African way of thinking and those who think as Europeans. (Let me note here that this writer has come to believe that the differences between the African system of thought and that which is Western or European is not solely dictated by place of birth or skin color in the current era but more importantly by how an individual responds to and uses the ideas inherent in each system. For I have known persons of European descent who have adapted the African system and persons of African descent who have adopted the European.)

She learned as a child in Jamaica "that food can be used as a weapon." She now understands that the slave trade developed Europe and led to the rise of the modern corporate/banking/government system. She states with the molten fire that bubbles below the surface of her understated persona:

. . . until we can teach our children to understand global power and its uses, we will not be successful . . . our dilemma is a power base that does not teach our children to understand . . . here and on the African continent . . . they [those that do understand] . . . reach a certain point and they are cut down . . .

She also said (and we need to listen closely to her):

. . . a middle-class system was created [by Europeans] . . . some [Africans] became millionaires . . . guns were supplied to initiate wars against the government and the people to allow the extraction of minerals from Africa . . .

"Unless," Sybil continues, "we [the African Diaspora] get together with people in Africa that see the light—it will take another fifty years to get there . . ."

One person who, without question, saw and shared the light and who was to become the focus of her existence was John Henrik Clarke. They had known each other for years from Pan-Africanist circles, such as the First World lectures in Harlem and trips to Egypt, one of which she was assigned to care for Dr. Clarke with another woman. His sight was failing.

At his request, Sybil started traveling with him in 1987. Sybil Williams and John Clarke found that they were ideological soul mates. The theme of John Clarke's life was Pan-Africanism. She remained a Garveyite and a committed Pan-Africanist. She understood his life and work, the fight for African People, and they had compatible views of African history.

They both believed in the uplifting of African people and their restoration to what John Clarke believed was their prominent place in world history.

They would travel to Egypt, London, and Ghana together. She states fervently, "John and Ben were rare human beings . . . they refused to compromise their principles . . . they paid a heavy price . . ."

"Nobody," Sybil states with a note of sadness at his pain and pride at his courage, "knows the suffering this man [Clarke] went through. She quotes him as saying, " . . . we live in a world of shadows, and I don't want to be a shadow."

In August of 1996, Sybil was with John Clarke when he met with Jerry Rawlings, the president of Ghana. Clarke discussed dual citizenship for Africans in the Diaspora, student exchanges, and reparation/debt reduction. They also met with the Queen Mother.

Frail, in ill health, and in the midst of a bitter divorce, Clarke's travels put him on a high; he would often sink into depression on his return to New York. Sybil Williams had taken care of John Clarke for twelve years. In 1997, his divorce final, Clarke asked Sybil to marry him. She did. He was to die on July 16, 1998.

Of their time together, Sybil Williams Clarke says somewhat wistfully, "That is another thing . . . people have to know what real meaningful love is . . . it is not just jumping in and out of bed with someone . . . that is part of it . . . the culmination of a love . . . a relationship . . . mutual respect . . . realism . . . that's when you know what real love is . . ."

Even in death, John Clarke remains a focused part of Sybil Williams Clarke's life. She wants to assure that his works are used in the manner that he intended. There is the John Clarke Institute, which now exists without walls, and his papers at the Schomburg Center in his beloved Harlem, Clarke House, and his book collection at Clark University in Atlanta.

Then there is her own work. She wants to write about Chief Nana Fre Fre, another influential person in the formulation of her thoughts.

Ever the activist, despite health challenges of her own, Sybil Williams Clarke, with the sound, rhythm, and spice of her Jamaican roots still evident, continues her lifetime of passionate struggle for self-determination while helping others and her people to see the light.

In sum: fire, steel, determination, knowledge, wisdom, loyalty, love, passion, dedication, truth, ethics, morality, honor, Maat—Sybil Williams Clarke. Warrior!

Doris Viola (Hobson) Osborne

Doris Viola (Hobson) Osborne

To listen to Doris Osborne as she sat in her home at 310 Greene Avenue in Brooklyn, New York, surrounded by the fruits of her productive life, reminded me of the time I heard the sea lapping against the rocks below my window the first morning I awoke in the Caribbean. At first, I couldn't identify what it was, for in the silence of the early morning, the power of the water was not easy to fathom. Once I got up and identified what it was, I returned to bed, and the rhythm lulled me back to sleep.

In much the same way, the power of Doris Osborne could be lost in the quiet simple way she spoke, often ending her statements with a self-depreciating chuckle. At times her chocolate-brown face crinkles, and her frail five-feet-two-inch, 140-pound, impeccably dressed frame would shake under the force of her robust laughter. But much like the power of the sea, she was truly something to be reckoned with. For she had seen and experienced much since she was born in Kings County Hospital in Brooklyn, New York, in 1919, to her parents, Charles and Miriam, both of whom were from Nevis in the then British West Indies.

At the time of her birth she was the only child, a brother and a sister having died before she was born. Her father and two of his brothers owned a cleaners and a tailor shop on Fulton Street in Brooklyn, which they lost during the Depression. Her mother, a seamstress, made lampshades at home.

Doris's loyalty to her Greene Avenue home was rooted in the sacrifices her parents made to acquire it. Two instances precipitated their move from Grand Avenue. In the first, a light-skinned Black family objected to Doris playing with their son and daughter. Every time Doris would come out to play, they would have their children go into the backyard of their home.

In the second incident, the Black superintendent of a building on Lexington Avenue lured Doris into the basement. Only the alertness of a neighbor kept Doris from being seriously harmed.

Thus, she came to Greene Avenue in 1927. Her family was one of the first, if not the first, Black family on the block. At that time, the neighborhood was Clinton Hills. It was inhabited mostly by Italians, Irish, and Jews. She remembered trolley cars running on Greene Avenue and a stable across the street for the horse-drawn buggies that were still in use. Doris attended the local schools. She said she did not experience discrimination from whites until she went to high school.

Doris attended Girls Commercial High School, where she studied typing and bookkeeping. It was here that she began to notice subtle differences in the way she was treated. She worked while in school as a babysitter and as a typist for a lawyer. Her ambition was to become a lawyer. Graduating at the top of her class, she applied for a typing job in 1936/1937 at a Wall Street firm.

The person in charge of hiring took Doris to the typing pool. Telling her to look around, he told her that none of the women typing there looked like her and that she would not fit in. Around the same time, Doris eloped with seventeen-year-old Joseph Allen Holmes. She was a year older then he was.

While courting, in order to bypass the objections of their parents, they would meet in my parents' home (my father John being a cousin to Doris) down the block from 310 Greene Avenue. The marriage lasted long enough for two children to be born—Kitty in 1938 and a son, Joseph Allen Jr., in 1947. Doris laughs now at how ignorant they both were to the facts of life. Doris did not know she was pregnant until she began getting sick on a swing in the park. A more knowledgeable woman explained to her what was going on.

That first marriage ended in divorce. Her husband was very abusive. Doris attributes this behavior in part to his being locked away when company came to his parents' home because his complexion was too dark. She said in retrospect—accepting her own responsibility for what transpired, without a trace of bitterness at the abusive relationship, but with some evident remorse—that if she had known it then and had been more mature and understanding, things might have worked out differently.

With two children to support, she used the skill she had learned from her seamstress mother to go to work in the garment industry. The work was seasonal; the pay was based on piecework. One Black woman at her first place of employment threatened to quit if Doris was hired. Doris was; the woman quit a week later.

In her first week, she made $3.50 for a forty-hour week. When she retired in 1981, after forty years of seasonal piecework, with a corresponding forty years in the International Ladies Garment Workers Union (ILGWU), she was making $150.00 a week. In her understated manner, Mrs. Osborne said, "the working conditions were not always pleasant." In addition to the work being seasonal (she soon learned to go from job to job according to the time of year, thus being able to work almost year-round), the machines were often placed next to drafty windows to make the best use of the available light.

Doris would sew in the factory by day and then make clothes for herself, her children, and others by night. She had become active in the union, having to join upon being employed at her first job in the garment industry. She eventually became a shop steward. The union now pays Doris her pension.

Doris was to marry for the second time. With her infectious laughter, she said, "I did not like him at first. He was a quiet, serious, responsible, churchgoing fella. I seemed to be drawn to the other type. But he was persistent." When she first married Vincent Osborne, he was the foreman in a jewelry factory. He was to eventually go to work in the post office when the factory went out of business.

Her whole being lit up when she spoke of this man, who died in 1987. An inner glow seemed to infuse her, and she visibly appeared to soften even more as she stated, in response to a question about the differences between her first and second husband, "Oh yes, this was a man." She tells of the time before they were married, when she was home sewing a coat for her son. Vinny saw what she was doing, stating that no son of his would ever again wear homemade clothes. He took the boy shopping and purchased him a coat.

There were no children born to Doris and Vincent as a result of their marriage. But both of Doris's children revered him as their father. So much so that the son wanted to change his last name to Osborne before he reached his majority. Doris prevented it in order for him to continue collecting the social security payments due him because of the death of his biological parent. Here was something else again that Doris stated with remorse. Years later, she was to learn how hurt her son was at this understandable action.

Throughout her life, Doris has been devoted to her family, community, and church. Her involvement in the community came about to a large degree by her estrangement from her church. She was born into the

Ebenezer Wesleyan Methodist Church. She states, "My mother used to pack food to take to church on Sunday. You knew you were going to be there all day."

(This was the same church my father attended, as did my brother, sister(s), and myself. Ebenezer was the family church of my youth.)

Doris became a Sunday-school teacher at the age of sixteen. She was strongly influenced by her grandfather, a Wesleyan Methodist minister in Nevis. Her parents had taught her to write letters to family members. Her grandfather was instrumental in instilling in her moral values. He died at the age of seventy-five. Yet she was to be excommunicated from her church at the time of her first marriage. She could not teach Sunday school nor sing in the choir. This angered her.

Stating "that life was just one big learning experience," Doris spoke of starting private singing lessons with Chauncey Northern Studios and then quitting because her first husband was jealous of the teacher. She then learned to play the organ. She felt that she "had to give something back" because she "was brought up that way."

Doris started working with food drives. She eventually returned to the church to become assistant organist. Doris resigned that position after it became clear to her that the senior organist began coming to church to play only on major holidays. Doris remained active in Ebenezer to her death.

Her community work led to her becoming active politically. Doris helped organize the Greene Avenue Block Association in 1955. She also worked in the campaign to elect Bertram Baker, a native Nevisan, as Brooklyn's first Black assemblyman. Now in addition to her church (she had dreams of establishing a cultural education center at the church), she works mostly with senior citizens. The clerical skills she learned in highschool that she was denied use of on Wall Street were used in her church when she became church secretary for twenty years, as well as secretary and president of her block association.

Under the influence of her faith, Doris has developed some clear thoughts on what it takes to make it in life. She said the impetus of having to raise two children moved her from being shy and passive. She had to survive in the garment industry and in life in general for the sake of her children and herself.

Doris stated she learned over the years that "everything would work out." Every time it did, her faith was reinforced to the point where she lived with that expectation.

Her passivity had evolved into a serenity borne out of years of living by the golden rule. She said, "I try to relate to people in a way that I would have them relate to me. In general I like people. I've tried to be friendly."

Doris continued, "As my parents did to me, I've instilled in my children not to do anything hurtful to anyone else, to try to forgive and to understand." (Her daughter, Kitty, is a successful artist; her son, Joe, a minister in Tennessee).

This does not mean that Doris Osborne had some Pollyanna view of the world. She was nothing else if not a realist about race and politics in the United States. She recalls quite clearly having to attend segregated movies in Asbury Park, New Jersey, in 1941-1942, where Blacks had to sit in the balcony separated from whites. She remembered when she went to see her daughter, Kitty, who was visiting relatives in the South during the civil rights movement, and learned that everywhere in the United States was not the same in racial matters.

From her vantage point on Greene Avenue, she had seen her neighborhood change from all white to all Black; she now sees that it is changing once more as whites begin to move in again. She, laughing, said that they keep moving the "rocks on her"—a reference to both the boundaries changing as the demographics change, as well as the fact that in the past, boundaries of towns and villages were often marked by deliberately placed rocks. Greene Avenue, at least for now, remains in Bedford-Stuyvesant.

(Interesting enough, this system of boundary marking with rocks or stones is also used in Africa.)

Ever mindful of the condition of Black Americans in the United States, she placed much of the responsibility for the state of Black people on themselves. Black people, she stated, could have taken better advantage of the hard-fought gains made by the civil rights movement.

Doris continued, saying, "I feel that once it [the law] was on the books, we should have moved in as a unit. There are still things here in Brooklyn we don't enjoy. Blacks were displaced by the new Atlantic Avenue Center, where I believe we have one store."

Doris Osborne, ever the activist, stated, "If we were more unified, we could have put our money together. We do not trust one another. We still have to frequent white establishments. She used the new Marriott Hotel in downtown Brooklyn as a recent example.

She was just as clear about the historic significance of skin color within and outside of the Black community. "Among your own," she stated, "it's stupidness. It affects you differently than from whites. Because of the power differences between Blacks and whites, some light-skinned Blacks feel closer to whites."

Mrs. Osborne said, "Because whites are more powerful in their affect on our daily lives, some of us look to the white man for our salvation. It is not going to happen."

The life of Doris Osborne, Aunt Doris to me and to many others, is testimony that character, faith in God, self, family, and people, along with laughter can lead to a consciousness that breeds serenity, which neither "stupidness" nor "power" can negate.

Doris Viola Osborne, quiet warrior, died on April 7, 2005.

Thank you, Aunt Doris.

Epilogue

These six women, in their hard-earned, self-defined individuality, are also painting in the similarities of their experiences as women of color a mural of the history of not only their generation but also of the history of our collective people.

It is no accident that these six women faced many of the same obstacles in defining themselves, first, as human beings and then as women and then as women of color. It did not matter whether they were in the United States, the Caribbean, or Europe. The color of their skin and their gender were seen by white supremacists—both male and female, and just as often, by misguided persons of color—as reason enough to deny them humanity, education, and jobs.

In their struggle are time-tested lessons for not only survival but also of not settling just for survival. Life dictated that they take control of themselves. They learned from the elders in their lives. They did not allow obstacles to deter them. They went around, over, under, and, when necessary, through them. Their will became their allies. Each success reinforced their faith in themselves. Their faith in themselves was, in turn, reinforced by their faith that they were being aided by a spirit inherent in them that was greater than themselves, even for those who did not belong to an organized church or religion or those who professed to be humanists, thus not believing in the spirit.

They learned who and what they were, knew where they came from, and identified where they wanted—often had—to go and would not allow anyone else to tell them otherwise.

Old folk say, "It ain't what you are called, it is what you answer to that matters."

Speaking of old folk, the elder, now ancestor, John Henrik Clarke taught us that history is a compass; it can tell you where you have been and where you are going. If you do not know where you have been, you will not know where you are, where you are going, or how to get there.

If you are ignorant of these principles, someone else—who may not have your best interest in mind—will surely show you the way. Such has been the case with people of color who allowed Europeans and their cohorts, many of whom are people of color, to show them the way.

History can and will repeat itself.

We must be relentless in our determination to keep the worst of history from repeating itself under different guises, but with the same results, our continued subjugation.

For in the starkest term, this is not so much a battle based on race, class, or gender. Nor was it, or is it, simply opposing ideologies or political differences. It was and continues to be nothing less than a conflict of contrasting worldviews.

On the one hand, the six women presented here embody the classic African and Native American indigenous people(s), communal, community view of sharing, a respect for nature, that is often interpreted as spirit.

On the other is the European mind-set, with its emphasis on individualism, dominance, and control of people and resources. Racism, class, and gender are divisive tools of this worldview cloaked in ideology, politics, and religion.

The weapons ruthlessly used in this war are religion (see Christianity and Islam), economics, and military and political power, to destroy people's belief in their culture, heritage, gods-and if they resist exterminating them.

As I have noted before, neither the attributes of the African worldview or that of the European have been shown to be exclusively confined to any one people. Acknowledging that is in itself a quantum leap in thinking for me. It has been a long journey from viewing the world almost exclusively in terms of Black and white to understanding it is more of thought and spirit. It is one of the more profound lessons I have learned from interacting with the people in this piece and others from the family of humanity.

But I have also come to believe that an implacable sense of purpose must be employed to resist the European mind-set as is employed by those implementing that mind-set around the globe.

One can argue strategy and tactics—but the proof of the imperative of resistance is in history.

Our six wonderful way showers came to understand that the struggle they fought was a continuation of a struggle from yesterday that goes on today and will continue into tomorrow. It is an intergenerational struggle.

What their lives teach us is that we, as individuals, have the inherent power to define ourselves—to resist domination—if we believe in ourselves, in our innate ability to empower self.

The first step in this resistance is the recognition of the existence of the ideology, the mind-set of dominance, of the use of the ruthless application of unbridled power to achieve goals and objectives, of the belief in the supremacy of the Western thought and culture above all others, regardless of what guises it is operating under. That first step should be followed by, but not limited to:

□ Arming yourself with the knowledge of who you are. Learn the history of your people. As John Henrik Clarke taught, this sometimes requires the reading of European writers and histories.
(The ancient Egyptians taught man and woman to know thy self.)

□ Look within your circle of family, friends, and community; and you will undoubtedly find examples of people who have overcome great odds to define themselves in a manner they are comfortable with.

□ Understand that the struggle of Africans, Native Americans, and people of color is/was a heroic one, and it continues unabated.

□ Know that you have a responsibility to those who came before you (the ancestors) and those who will follow you (the future) to engage in resistance in a manner that you are comfortable with (now).

The lives of the women/warriors profiled here embody the elements of resistance.

Their power is that they know/knew that no one is going to empower us. In life, you must be prepared to take what is rightfully yours, to demand-self definition, using the gifts the universe has provided all of us.

What moved these women from the ordinary to the extraordinary was their recognition that it was so despite what all of the naysayers did and said.

Postscript

And so this ends . . . the torch was passed to these women by those who preceded them . . . as they now pass it to those of us who follow them . . . as it will be passed to those who come after us . . . so it has always been . . . and so it will always be . . . as long as there is a need for the struggle to continue . . .

Peace,
Bernard W. Saunders
Sarasota, Florida
July 28, 2007

www.ingramcontent.com/pod-product-compliance
Lightning Source LLC
Chambersburg PA
CBHW050338290526
45785CB00006B/2541